MAGIC TRICKS

CARD MAGIC

Written by
JOHN WOOD

W9-BWQ-570

Gareth Stevens
PUBLISHING

Please visit our website, www.garethstevens.com.
For a free color catalog of all our high-quality books,
call toll free 1-800-542-2595 or fax 1-877-542-2596.

Cataloging-in-Publication Data

Names: Wood, John.
Title: Card magic / John Wood.
Description: New York : Gareth Stevens Publishing, 2019. | Series: Magic tricks | Includes glossary and index.
Identifiers: LCCN ISBN 9781538225967 (pbk.) | ISBN 9781538225950 (library bound) |
ISBN 9781538225981 (6 pack)
Subjects: LCSH: Card tricks--Juvenile literature.
Classification: LCC GV1549.W663 2019 | DDC 793.85--dc23

First Edition

Published in 2019 by
Gareth Stevens Publishing
111 East 14th Street, Suite 349
New York, NY 10003

© 2018 Booklife Publishing
This edition is published by arrangement with Booklife Publishing

Produced for Gareth Stevens by Booklife
Editor: Kirsty Holmes
Designer: Danielle Jones

Picture credits: Cover & 1 – Pretty Vectors. 2 – LiliGraphie, Oksana Shufrych, Kat_Branch, Katja
Gerasimova, chelovector. 3 – fox18002, Macrovector. 4 – MBR9292, alicedaniel, 12photography. 5 –
Everett - Art, Chepko Danil Vitalevich. 6 – Freedom_Studio, Aaron Amat, FeelIFree, a_bachelorette.
7 – Tatiana Popova, Ann Worthy. 8 – Featureflash Photo Agency, Frame Art, janniwet, rangizzz, Katja
Gerasimova, Harry Houdini [Public domain], via Wikimedia Commons. 9 – kocetoiliev, kolotuschenko.
10 – Tatiana Popova, Prostock-studio, Champion studio, Vera Petruk. 11 – elbud, Croisy, Tatiana Popova.
12 – LiliGraphie, AngeloDeVal, chronicler. 13 – Ian Dikhtiar. 14 – cpg-photo, supercavie, Peter Kotoff. 15
– supercavie, Mu-ta-bor, Jan Kowalski, bogdan ionescu, Ekachai Sathittaweechai, Olga Rutko. 16 – Nejron
Photo, Dmytro Surkov. 17 – Aaron Amat, Africa Studio, SCOTTCHAN. 18 – Jaroslaw Saternus, Zvereva
Iana, Frank Boott Goodrich (1826-1894) and Jules Champagne [Public domain], via Wikimedia Commons.
19 – Africa Studio. 20 – bnamfa, Prachaya Roekdeethaweesab, Aleem Zahid Khan, Ekachai Sathittaweechai.
22 – ZioDave (http://www.flickr.com/photos/ziodave/25510393) [CC BY-SA 2.0 (https://creativecommons.
org/licenses/by-sa/2.0)], via Wikimedia Commons, Nikki (IMG_1374) [CC BY 2.0 (http://creativecommons.
org/licenses/by/2.0)], via Wikimedia Commons. 23 – Aleem Zahid Khan. 24 – bobyramone, Mercurio,
Auttapon Wongtakeaw. 25 – NShu. 26 – viewgene, Early Spring. 27 – Thirteen. 28 – Lutsin Yury, Jackie
Smithson. 29 – Africa Studio, Prostock-studio. 30 – Rosli Othman.
Images are courtesy of Shutterstock.com. With thanks to Getty Images, Thinkstock Photo and iStockphoto.

All rights reserved. No part of this book may be reproduced in any form
without permission from the publisher, except by a reviewer.

Printed in the United States of America

CPSIA compliance information: Batch #CS18GS:
For further information contact Gareth Stevens, New York, New York at 1-800-542-2595.

CARD MAGIC
CONTENTS

Words that look like **this** are explained in the glossary on page 31.

CAN YOU KEEP A SECRET?

So, you want to be a magician? Well, you've come to the right place. There are many secrets waiting for you inside this book. By the time you're finished reading, you will be a master of card magic. Let's begin!

CARDS

This is a pack of playing cards. Some cards have numbers on them, from two to ten. Some have pictures, which are called jacks, queens, or kings. Four of the cards, which represent the number one, are called aces.

Each card also has a suit:

Diamonds

Clubs

Hearts

Spades

DID YOU KNOW?
There are
52
cards in a standard <u>deck</u>.

4

THE HISTORY OF CARD MAGIC

Card magic has been **performed** for hundreds of years. Cards are one of the most famous magic **props** in history. Lots of magicians have a deck of cards ready in case they need to amaze an audience!

Modern-day playing cards became popular around the year 1500 in France.

Nowadays, card magic is performed all over the world. You might see card magic being performed on the street, at a magic show, or at a party.

DID YOU KNOW?

It is thought that the first playing cards were invented in China thousands of years ago.

MAGIC LESSON:
CUTTING CARDS
AND THE
RIFFLE SHUFFLE

CUTTING CARDS

Cutting a deck means to take a top chunk of cards and put it at the bottom. The chunk of top cards can be as big or as small as you like.

STEP 1

Using your thumb and finger, take a chunk of cards from the top.

STEP 2

Put it to the side of the deck.

STEP 3

Take the cards that are left and put them on top of the chunk. This is called completing the cut.

THE RIFFLE SHUFFLE

Shuffling cards means putting them all in a <u>random</u> order. This is easier to do on a table or the floor.

STEP 1

Split the cards into two piles, one in each hand. Hold each pile with your thumb under one end and your fingers under the other.

STEP 2

Bend each pile up with your thumbs and put them closer together, almost in an "A" shape.

STEP 3

Gently ease your thumbs upwards, so that the ends of the cards flick downwards. Cards from each pile should <u>overlap</u> each other so they are all mixed up.

MIND READER

Our first trick is all about reading minds. Or, at least, making people think that you can read minds. <u>Mentalists</u>, like Derren Brown, are famous for <u>convincing</u> an audience that they can read thoughts just by looking into someone's eyes.

Derren Brown's tricks often use <u>suggestions</u> to put an idea in the audience's heads. For example, he might use words to do with bicycles, without the audience realizing. Then, when he asks the audience to think of an object, they think of a bicycle. Now he can tell them what they were thinking of.

Derren Brown

Jean-Eugène Robert-Houdin

DID YOU KNOW?

Some of the earliest known mind-reading tricks were performed by Jean-Eugène Robert-Houdin, who was a great magician.

YOU WILL NEED...

Paper

Cards

Pencil

REMEMBER, this trick is all about convincing your audience you are actually reading their mind. Make sure you put on a big show with your best acting!

STEP 1

Shuffle the cards. Afterwards, go through the cards <u>faceup</u>, showing the audience that they are shuffled.

STEP 2

While going through the cards, look to see what the bottom card facing up is. Remember this card!

Remember the last card!

STEP 3

Put the deck <u>facedown</u>. The card you memorized will now be the card on top. Ask your audience to make a cut, anywhere they like.

This is the card you remembered.

STEP 4

Once they have put a chunk of cards to the side, pick up the cards that are left, <u>rotate</u> them sideways and put them half on top, like this.

STEP 5

Explain to your audience that, soon, they will take a card and then you are going to read their mind.

STEP 6

Take away the sideways cards from the top. Now ask the audience to take the top card of the pile that is left. Ask them to remember it and not to show you.

STEP 7

Pretend to read their mind! Then write down the card that you remembered earlier on the piece of paper.

STEP 8

Put the paper and their card facedown in the middle. Turn them over to reveal that they are the same!

FIND YOUR CARD

Audiences love this trick. First, someone picks a card from the deck. Without looking, the magician places the chosen card back in the deck in a random spot. After a bit of mixing and a bit of magic, the chosen card is found!

"Find the card" tricks are very old. Some go back as far as the 1800s.

DID YOU KNOW?

Magicians like Ricky Jay are famous for their card magic tricks. Almost all of Ricky Jay's magic tricks use a deck of cards.

Ricky Jay

YOU WILL NEED...

A standard
deck of cards

THIS TRICK

uses a key card. A key card is
a normal card that helps you
find another card. Once you
know where the key card is,
it means the next card will
be the chosen card.

STEP 1

Shuffle the cards. Afterwards, go through the cards faceup, showing the audience that they are shuffled.

STEP 2

While going through the cards, remember what the top card facing up is. This is the key card, so remember it!

STEP 3

Now, flip the deck facedown. <u>Fan</u> the cards out and ask them to pick a card and remember it without showing you.

STEP 4

Put this card on the top of the deck.

STEP 5

Make and complete a few cuts. You can let the audience make a cut if they want.

STEP 6

Explain that you are going to take cards from the top, one by one, and turn them over. You are going to use magic to "sense" when the chosen card is coming up.

STEP 7

Now take the top card from the deck and place it faceup in a pile. Keep doing this until you see the key card you remembered before.

STEP 8

Without turning it over, place the next card facedown and remove the rest of the cards. Flip it over to reveal the chosen card!

MAGIC LESSON:
CARD HANDLING
AND
FORCING CARDS

CARD HANDLING

It is a good idea to practice as much as you can so that you look **confident**. If you look confident, people won't notice all the special magician's secrets you are using!

FORCING CARDS

Sometimes in magic, you might need to make the audience choose a certain card without them knowing about it. This is called forcing a card.

DID YOU KNOW?

Professional magicians use very complicated hand movements to force cards on people. This is called sleight of hand.

The double-cut force is a move that forces the top card onto the audience. Here's how you do it:

STEP 1

Start by placing your deck of cards facedown. When doing this in a trick, you will have already memorized what the top card is. Now make a shallow cut, taking just a few cards from the top of the deck.

STEP 2

Flip this top chunk over so the cards are facing up and put it on top of the other cards.

STEP 3

Make a deeper cut picking up a lot more cards than you did before.

STEP 4

Flip this new chunk over, like you did before, so that the cards are faceup and put it on top of the other cards.

STEP 5

Tell the audience that that they will remove the top cards, which are faceup, and take the first card facing down. The first card facing down will still be the one you memorized at the beginning of this trick.

THE THREE-CARD PREDICTION TRICK

History tells many tales of fortune-tellers who could see into the future with their crystal balls. In a <u>prediction</u> card trick, the magician seems to look into the future to guess what cards the audience will choose. The cards are revealed at the end, and the magician has guessed them all right!

DID YOU KNOW?

Marie-Anne Adelaide Lenormand was a famous fortune-teller who lived in France around 1800. She was incredibly rich, and people would come from all over Europe to see her.

Marie-Anne Adelaide Lenormand

A standard
deck of cards

WHEN MAKING

your predictions, you might
want to **hesitate** a little longer,
as if you are really thinking
about it. This will make it
more convincing.

In this trick we talk about matching cards.
A matching card has the same color and number,
or picture, but a different suit. So, if the audience
picks a 6 of hearts, the matching card is the 6
of diamonds.

STEP 1

Shuffle the cards. Afterwards, go through the cards faceup, showing the audience that they are shuffled. While going through the cards, make a note of the last card and remember it!

This is the last card.

STEP 2

Explain that you are going to predict which cards will be chosen. Hold up the cards so the audience can only see the backs. Choose the matching card to your remembered card and put it facedown to the left.

This is the matching card: the jack of spades.

STEP 3

Fan the cards out facedown, and ask the audience to pick a card. Put their chosen card faceup next to your prediction on the left.

STEP 4

Now make another prediction. Pick the matching card to the one the audience just chose and put it facedown in the middle. Let the audience pick another card. Put it next to your middle prediction.

This is the matching card to the five of hearts: the five of diamonds.

STEP 5

Make another prediction, picking the matching card of the facing-up middle card. Put it facedown to the right.

STEP 6

Now ask your audience to pick their last card and use the double-cut force. Put the forced card next to the right prediction.

STEP 7

Using your right hand, put the cards on top of each other from right to left. Pick the pile up and count the cards into your left hand, one on top of the other. When you get to the last card, move it to the bottom of the pile.

STEP 8

Deal the cards left to right in three groups. Each group should have one card facing up and one card facing down. Now reveal the matching cards in each group!

FOLLOW
THE LEADER

In this trick, you will make two piles of cards switch places without even touching them. In the past, performers of street magic would use tricks to switch cards all the time. An audience would try and guess which card was their chosen card. However, the performers had already switched the cards – so the audience guessed wrong every time!

Street Magic

DID YOU KNOW?

David Blaine is a famous magician who performs lots of street card magic.

David Blaine

YOU WILL NEED...

The four queens of each suit, which you've set aside from the deck.

The rest of the deck of cards

DURING THIS TRICK,
you will need to flip a card over with another card. Try to make this look <u>casual</u>. Make sure you practice so you get it right the first time in front of an audience.

STEP 1

Lay the four queens next to each other facing down. Deal three random cards on each of the queens. You should have four piles.

STEP 2

Put the piles on top of each other, from right to left.

STEP 3

Count through the pile, still facing down. The order is "card, card, card, queen, card, card, card, queen," and so on. Each time you get to a queen, you can quickly show your audience the card, to prove it is the queen.

STEP 4

Deal the top four cards of the pile in your hands in a row from right to left. Use the next top card and use it to flip the left-most card over. It should be a queen. Now put the card you used for flipping at the bottom of the deck in your hand. Turn the flipped queen facedown again.

STEP 5

Keep dealing the cards from right to left until you run out then remove the two piles on the right.

  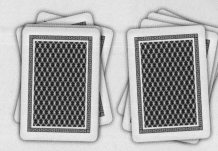

STEP 6

Take the bottom card from the left remaining pile and put it in front of the left pile. It should be a queen. Do the same for the right pile. It should be random.

STEP 7

Swap the two cards that are facing up so the queen is now on the right. Explain that you are going to use magic to swap the piles facing down, so that they follow their leader.

STEP 8

Snap your fingers and reveal the piles. The piles should have switched too!

25

MAGIC LESSON:
THE HINDU SHUFFLE

The Hindu shuffle is a special way of shuffling cards. Here's how you do it:

STEP 1

Using your right hand, place your thumb on one side of the deck and your fingers on the other. Make sure you've got a good grip on the bottom cards.

STEP 2

Take your left hand and place it palm-up. Using the thumb and middle finger of the left hand, take a small chunk of cards from the top of the deck and let them drop into your left palm.

STEP 3

Keep doing this until you've gone through the whole deck.

STEP 4

When you get to the last few cards, place them on top of the cards in your left palm.

26

THE HINDU SHUFFLE FORCE

The Hindu shuffle force is a bit different from the Hindu shuffle because you can use it to force a card on an audience. Take a note of the bottom card. It won't matter when they shout stop, the bottom card is always the same.

STEP 1 Start doing the Hindu shuffle.

STEP 2 Ask your audience to call out "STOP!" whenever they want.

STOP!

STOP!

STOP!

STEP 3

When they shout "stop," stop shuffling the cards. Turn the cards in your right hand faceup. This card will be the bottom card that you remembered earlier.

THE CHANGING-COLOR CARD TRICK

Our last trick is very beautiful. We are going to change the back of a card to a different color. You will be using the Hindu shuffle force, so make sure you've practiced!

YOU WILL NEED...

One card with a blue-colored back that is secretly put to the bottom of the deck

A full deck of cards with a red-colored back

TRY TO
do the Hindu shuffle as quickly as possible, so the audience doesn't know what is really happening.

You need to remember what number and suit the blue card is. Remove the red-backed version of this card from your deck. Do this in secret.

STEP 1

Fan out a few of the top cards, showing the red-colored backs. This shows the audience that there is nothing unusual about your pack of cards.

STEP 2

Do the Hindu shuffle force making sure that the blue-backed card is the bottom card. Ask the audience to stay "STOP!" when they want.

STEP 3

Flip one hand over when the audience says stop. This is their chosen card.

This card should have a blue back.

29

STEP 4

Take the chosen card and put it faceup in front of the audience. Don't let them see the back.

STEP 5

Spread the other cards out facedown and explain you are going to magically change the back of their chosen card.

STEP 6

Snap your fingers. Turn the card over and show them it has a blue-colored back.

PRACTICE

all these tricks until you can amaze your friends and family. And remember, don't let them see this book. A true magician never reveals their secrets!

GLOSSARY

casual	natural and normal-looking
confident	feeling good about yourself and believing that you will do something well
convincing	making people believe something is true
deal	set out or give out cards one by one
deck	a full set of cards
facedown	when the card's back is pointing up
faceup	when the card's number or picture is pointing up
fan	spread the tops of the cards out in a fan shape while holding the bottoms in place
hesitate	pause before doing or saying something you are not sure about
mentalists	magicians who do mind magic
overlap	when two or more things cover each other slightly
performed	put on a show for an audience
prediction	a guess about something that is going to happen in the future
props	objects used to help with a show
random	something that happens without a plan or order
rotate	to spin or wheel around in one place
suggestions	ideas given to a person to think about

INDEX